So You Want To Start Keeping Chickens?

A Real Beginner's Guide

By Mark Burrows

Copyright

Title: So You Want To Start Keeping Chickens

Author: Mark Burrows

First Published in 2012

Redlynch Farm, Main Road, Stickney, Boston, Lincolnshire, PE22 8EQ

ISBN 978-1-4717-9322-6

Book design: Colette Mason

Editing: Valerie Warner

Table of Contents

Foreword

First of all, let me say that you have made a very wise choice in buying this book which is going to give you all the information you need to know to enable you to get started in this great hobby.

So as a special thank you I would like you to scan the QR Code or visit http://www.chickens-for-sale.com/free-gift and you will be taken to a special, secret page where there is a surprise FREE gift waiting just for you.

Thanks for the people who helped me.

Although I myself have written this book, it would not have been possible without the help and support of some truly wonderful people who have helped me, so I would just like to take this opportunity to thank them.

I would like to thank Mark Mooney, Jo Barnes, Chris Farrell, Nick James, my many fantastic followers on Facebook and my family and friends for encouraging me to write this book in the first place.

The star of the show has been my friend and mentor, Colette Mason, who was my guide right through the whole process and has been a pillar of support when things got tough, as well as doing all the design work for the book. Without Colette I'm not sure the book would ever have been finished.

I would also like to thank Valerie Warner for her patience and skill in editing the book.

Thank you also to my darling wife, Sharon, who shares my passion for keeping chickens and whose contribution and support have been tremendous.

Finally my first 3 chickens, George, Gertie and Mabel.

Mark Burrows, Lincolnshire, 2012

Introduction

First of all let me extend a very warm welcome to my book, So You want to Start Keeping Chickens?

My name is Mark and together with my wife Sharon we have been keeping chickens for over 25 years, it has been a great journey.

Mark Burrows

Keeping chickens is a practice that dates back as far as when people started keeping animals.

They are fun to have around, make great pets and are low maintenance.

If you have space in your back garden the idea of keeping a few chickens may have occurred to you, but maybe you felt that you needed some more information before you got started, well this book will give you all the information you need

More and more people are now starting to keep a few chickens in their garden or backyard, there is nothing more gratifying than watching your happy chickens roaming free, scratching around without a care in the world. They just seem to add that little bit of magic to the garden.

On top of that, children absolutely adore chickens as they make super friendly pets, as an added bonus they provide fresh eggs and you know exactly what has gone into each egg and that it's been laid by a very happy hen.

For the last couple of years many of my friends, family, customers, not to mention my fans on Facebook, have said I should write a book on how to get started in this great hobby, namely "Keeping Chickens".

It was felt that a new breed of book was needed that everyone who wants to keep a few chickens in their garden can afford to buy, while at the same time gives all the information required by the beginner to be able to set up, purchase, handle and look after their chickens properly to ensure they remain fit and healthy.

That book should contain all that is really valuable to the person who keeps chickens for pleasure.

It should be written in plain easy to understand English and be practical and simple.

It should be a plain and truthful talk between writer and reader and in answer to this demand I offer my humble little book, all of which is respectfully submitted to the reader.

What this book covers

Before writing this book I decided that as well as calling on my 25 years experience of keeping chickens I would do some research and carry out some surveys to find out exactly what beginners to chicken keeping wanted to know from such a book.

I have listed some points below that are included in the book to ensure you have all the information you need to know to get started in this wonderful hobby.

Chapter 1
Benefits Of Keeping Chickens

In the opening chapter I shall outline and explain some of the great benefits of keeping chickens, such as they make great pets, give you lots of eggs, fun to have around and children absolutely adore them.

Chapter 2
Doing The Groundwork

Before you get your chickens it is very important to do the ground work beforehand, this will save you loads of problems further down the line. I shall cover all the information you will need to get you started on the right track.

Chapter 3
Feeding Your Chickens

Understanding the importance of making sure your chickens get the correct diet to maintain good health and vigour.

I will cover the different types of food feeders, drinkers, how much to feed, treats and all the information you need to feed your chickens properly.

Chapter 4
Choosing And Getting Your First Chickens

At first this could give you quite a headache as there are many different types and breeds of chicken to choose from. The information given in this chapter will cover the different breeds and types that I believe are suitable for a beginner and will tell you how to obtain your hens and where to get them from.

This chapter will ensure that you get the right chickens for you.

Chapter 5
Looking After Your Chickens

This chapter will cover everything you need to know to help you look after your chickens on a day-to-day basis.

I will go through getting your hens home and settling them in, routine maintenance, feeders, drinkers and how to cope with severe weather conditions, how to overcome problems and hints and tips to make your life easier.

Chapter 6
Poultry Problems And Diseases

I will explain that by looking after your chickens properly in the first place, problems and diseases should be few and far between.

I have, however, covered some of the more common problems that you could encounter at some stage of your journey with chickens.

Chapter 7
Frequently Asked Questions From Our Facebook Page

I have included in this chapter some of the frequently asked questions from our Facebook page "I Love Keeping Chickens". The questions are from beginners, just like you, and they will help solve some of the problems you may encounter along the way.

Resource Section

I thought it would be a good idea to provide you with a few good reference points to help you find good suppliers, organisations, useful websites and magazines.

So without any further ado, let's get started ☺

Benefits Of Keeping Chickens

The benefits of keeping chickens are numerous and varied. Here are just a few examples of how these wonderful little creatures can enhance our lives.

- They produce eggs.
- They make excellent pets.
- They can save you money.
- They are therapeutic.

Fresh Eggs

Having your own hens means that you have home produced fresh eggs. These eggs will come from hens that are fed and looked after by you. This way you have the comfort of knowing what they are fed on and the environment in which they are being kept. In this day and age of additives, artificial growth promoters and chemicals it is good to have a food product that contains none of these things.

You will also be safe in the knowledge that your eggs have come from your own "Happy Hens" and not from caged battery hens.

Even though the regulations have changed as of 01 January 2012 with regards to the types of cages the hens are kept in, the new ones are still far from ideal. It is my own opinion that all chickens should have the opportunity to be able to go outside where they can express their natural behaviour and have a good scratch around.

Great Tasting Eggs

Chickens As Pets

Chickens make fantastic pets, although hens are a better choice for this purpose. If you are a novice to the world of chickens or have young children, avoid buying or taking on a cockerel. They can be tricky to handle and can be quite aggressive.

Hens on the other hand are docile creatures and can become very friendly. They make ideal pets for children and will introduce them to the world of responsibility. It also puts them in touch with where their food comes from.

Schools up and down the country now keep a few hens on the grounds of the school for these teaching opportunities. Children really enjoy looking after them and especially collecting the eggs.

Money Saving

It is cheaper to keep a few hens to produce your own eggs than it is to buy them from a shop or supermarket.

A hen can produce up to 300 eggs in her first year, although she will lay a few less in her second and subsequent years. You will need at least two hens, preferably three as they like company of their own kind and do not do well on their own.

You will have surplus eggs now and again to either sell from your gate or supply to friends and family. If you sell some of your eggs it will help with the cost of the feed.

Chicken poo and the soiled straw or wood shavings that are cleared from the coop provide valuable material for your compost heap. Rotted down it is high in nitrogen and can be used on your veg or flower garden. It has no unpleasant odour once rotted and will feed your soil to give you marvellous home grown veg.

Chickens also have labour saving qualities. They will clear any ground that you put them on in just over a week. They will either eat or scratch up the grass and weeds and consume numerous bugs, pests, small slugs and snails.

All you have to do is move the chickens to another spot and plant your veg where they have cleared. This way they are saving you money on your feed as well by supplementing themselves with nutritious tit bits from the ground.

Free Fertiliser

The waste products of your chickens can be utilized as fertilisers. It has always been noted in many sources that chicken waste is one of the best fertilisers around for its high amount of nutrients and nitrogen that can help your garden produce vegetables at a faster rate, also the fact that they're organic (if they are fed organically) makes your crops free from harmful chemicals. It's also a plus that your chickens feed on bugs and insects that incessantly wreak havoc on your crops.

Chickens Are Therapeutic

No matter how stressful a day you have had, spending some time with your chooks will soon make you forget the strains of the day and it's much cheaper than a therapist!

Each chicken has its own little character and they can be so amusing. We spend time everyday with our chickens watching them and their antics, before you know where you are an hour has disappeared and you have to get back to the job's you were supposed to be doing!!

Spending some time with your chickens everyday is essential so you become familiar with each other. Once they get to know you they will rush to greet you to see if you have a treat for them.

You will also become familiar with what is normal chicken behaviour so you can spot immediately if something is wrong and deal with it promptly.

Chookie Checkpoint

The humble chicken was once considered a sacred animal symbolic of the sun

Summary

As you can see there are many benefits to keeping a few chickens in your garden and I am sure you will discover even more as you start keeping your own.

Having the initiative to learn more and taking a humane approach to keeping chickens can pave the way to maximizing these benefits, and both you and your avian family will be happier for it.

Now we have looked at some of the benefits in keeping chickens, I know that you will be itching to get cracking.

In the next chapter we are going to take a look at a few things you need to be aware of before you actually get your first chickens.

Doing The Groundwork

You are probably now getting very excited about getting your hens, but before you rush out and buy them there are certain things you need to think about, and measures you need to put in place first to ensure your chicken-keeping venture is relatively problem free.

Without further ado, let's have a look at some of the groundwork you'll need to do.

- Getting permissions
- Build or buy your coop
- Build your own chicken coop
- Buying considerations

Getting Permissions

Generally speaking, there are no restrictions on keeping small numbers of chickens in your garden or backyard. It is only if you keep more than 50 here in the UK that you must register the flock with DEFRA as it is then deemed to be a commercial enterprise.

You should check that there are no clauses in the deeds to your house that state you must not keep chickens on the property. Occasionally, even if there is such a clause it may have been there so long that it no longer applies anyway.

If you live in local authority housing or rented property you should check with your council or landlord to make sure you are allowed to keep chickens. Also it may be worth approaching your neighbours to tell them what you are proposing and maybe drop into the conversation that there may be some free eggs coming their way, this should get them onboard.

If you live in the city you should not consider getting a cockerel or rooster, they can be very noisy and will be sure to annoy your neighbours, resulting in complaints.

A Sussex Hybrid Chicken

Build Or Buy Your Coop

Now we have done our research and have established that you can keep chickens in your garden legally, the next most important thing we have to consider is where your chickens are going to live.

The 2 main options you have is to build a chicken coop yourself or, if funds permit you can buy a readymade one that suits your purposes, so let's have a look at those options in a bit more detail.

Build Your Own Chicken Coop

So, you're planning on building a chicken coop but don't know how to go about it? Don't worry.

You're about to get information on various chicken coop plans, designs, building materials, chicken breeds and what factors to consider before you get down to building your own chicken coop and how to construct it.

Instead of spending hundreds of pounds or dollars on a readymade chicken coop, you can now save on at least 50% of the cost by constructing it yourself! It's one of the best investments you can make that not only makes economic sense, but keeps giving rich dividends through the year - your food scraps get recycled, your backyard becomes bug and weed free and you even get a rich fertilizer!

Congratulations on a decision well made! Building a chicken coop can be a great weekend project that's both enjoyable and rewarding. It's something you can be proud of and reap the benefits of for years to come.

Imagine getting fresh, tasty and healthy eggs from your own backyard! Not to mention new pets who are extremely social and make for the most natural sounding alarm clock!

What's more, by raising chickens you've done your bit towards stopping the cruel treatment meted out on them in commercial battery cages where these poor birds are crammed into small spaces and don't even have enough room to turn their heads!

The good thing is, thousands of people have built their own chicken coops successfully so you know it's absolutely doable, especially if you have a good plan and design to follow!

As you know, chickens need a warm place to live through the year, a place that keeps them safe from predators and shelters them from bad weather and cold air drafts. Known as chicken coops, chicken houses or chicken shacks; they are structures where chickens are housed that can be built on a homestead or backyard of a house.

Most chicken coops are made of wood,using basic tools and materials that don't call for a big investment. You even have the option of building a chicken coop with materials found at your home!

The most important thing to consider before you start with the construction is a proper plan and design. There are many kinds of plans and designs available online, so you might want to check them out.

Factors To Consider

With proper planning, you can save on money and time. Know exactly what you want in terms of design, the size of the chicken coop, the number of chickens you plan on keeping and what kind of breed. In your eagerness to get started, don't rush through the planning stage.

After all, the idea is to build a safe, sturdy and well constructed chicken coop so you can raise healthy chickens that lay lots of delicious eggs and planning is critical to getting it right in the first shot! So before you decide on a design and start building the chicken coop, do keep these factors in mind:

Type

All types and sizes of chicken coop plans and designs are available, ranging from two storey structures to simple doghouse varieties, from mobile to stationary chicken coops. You first need to decide on the type of chicken coop you want to build based on the number of chickens you plan on keeping.

Dimensions

Whether you need a small, medium or large sized chicken coop depends on the space needed to house each chicken. A safe measurement is 4 square feet of space per chicken, this will provide them plenty of room to scratch and roam around. It's always better to err on the side of extra space when it comes to the size of a chicken coop since overcrowding can lead to illness, fights and unhappy birds.

Also, do keep some space for the waterers and feeders inside the coop.

Location

Decide on a portion of land where you plan on building the chicken coop, then check out the ground saturation. If the land tends to collect water it doesn't make for a good location. In case you reside in the city, make sure to look up its regulations regarding chicken coops as in some areas you need to build them 5 feet away from the property's boundary. It makes sense to position the coop on a spot that's dry, properly ventilated and visible from your home so you'll know if there's any trouble brewing, but not too close since chickens can get a little noisy sometimes.

Style

Ensure that your chicken coop looks good in your garden and doesn't stick out like a sore thumb or eye sore! Choose a design that matches your property and even enhances its value. You might want to use the same paint color used on your home's doors and windows.

Structure

It's important that the coop doesn't get too drafty or cold for the chickens. Cold winds will make the chickens uncomfortable, which in turn will slow their egg production.

Cleaning

Keep in mind that you'll need to clean the coop often, so make sure it's easy to clean and enter. You'll also need to get in to collect eggs, so make the coop tall enough for you to easily go in. Avoid keeping the floor level or you'll have an accumulated pool of water every time you wash it. The way out is to give a slight tilt to the floor as well as a slant leading out the back door.

Climate

It is also crucial for the coop to be built according to the climate of the area you live in. If the weather is warm through the year, use wire doors and walls to ensure there is plenty of ventilation so your chickens are kept cool. If you live in a cold climate, build solid walls to keep out cold winds, rain and snow, and take care that the drinking water doesn't freeze over. You can achieve this by insulating the walls while also ensuring good ventilation, since it's important that fresh air drifts in and out of the coop. If it rains frequently in your area, try building the chicken coop in a spot protected by trees, thereby reducing direct rain from hitting it.

Protection

Figure out which predators are potential threats to your chickens depending on where you live. Is there a problem of hawks, coyotes, raccoons, skunks, foxes, bears, fisher cats, lions or rodents? You need to take various preventative measures depending on the type of predators. Remember, your chicken's protection is entirely in your hands. A solid chicken wire fencing that's one foot deep and all along the boundary is essential. To deal with digging predators, you can partly bury the fence 8 to 12 inches below the ground, plus you should be able to lock them in at night.

Chicken Coop Plans

When it comes to chicken coop plans they're either too complicated or inaccurate, so take care while selecting yours! The right plan is critical for your chickens safety, productivity and overall wellbeing. Choosing your chicken coop plan will depend entirely on your specific needs. If you're planning on keeping one or two birds you can go for a portable chicken coop, also known as chicken tractors or arks.

A Chicken Tractor or Ark

This style is ideal for cities since it is mobile and doesn't have a floor. As a result, you can easily shift it from one part of your lawn to another.

Another advantage is that chicken droppings make for a great fertilizer and chickens love feeding on insects, so you'll have healthy, verdant grass!

This A-shaped structure with sides covered by wire fencing is easy to clean, carry, maintain and construct!

You can conveniently keep an eye over the birds in this portable chicken coop.

It is by far the safest mobile chicken enclosure that allows your birds to roam around freely while keeping them protected from prowling predators.

If you add wheels to your chicken tractor it becomes even more mobile, just make sure to attach water pans and feeders to the chicken tractor before you start moving it!

- You will need to fence the area around it with meshed wire that is around 15mm in diameter and bury it 30 cm under the ground.

- Keep at least four square feet of space for each chicken.

- Don't forget to build a chicken roost inside the chicken tractor, so your chickens have a place to sleep.

- Place a plastic sheet under the rooster to collect chicken droppings.

As you can imagine, a chicken tractor won't cost you much as long as you use a good plan.

Backyard Chicken Coops

This option is extremely popular in rural areas, while the small ones are more suited to city life with its space restrictions. Backyard chicken coops are usually open structured coops surrounded by fences in the form of a yard, so the chickens can roam around freely while getting plenty of ventilation. However, building and using small backyard coops instead of large ones is becoming increasingly popular:

- Small chicken coops are better suited to busy and hectic lifestyles.

- More and more families are keeping chickens in their urban backyards where large coops are just not practical.

- A small coop looks nice in the garden while also providing fresh, organic eggs.

- It is easy to clean and maintain. While the chickens are out for a stroll, you can clean it in 20 minutes flat!

- They aren't inferior to large chicken coops, just smaller in size. The materials used are just as high quality, long lasting and strong as those used to build large shelters.

While finalizing a small backyard chicken coop plan, make sure that it factors in:

- Cost effectiveness

- Ease of cleaning

- Provides safety from predators

- Entrance size

- Number of windows

- Good quality material

- Adequate space

- Fits nicely and aesthetically in your backyard

- Has perches

Most people assume that building a chicken coop requires a lot of money and is a difficult task. Truth is the construction is easy once you have the right plan that's made to scale and has cross sectional pictures of the coop.

You don't have to be an expert carpenter to construct a successful chicken coop, plus it's a great way to use your weekend productively and creatively! If it's your first chicken coop, keep the design simple and choose one online rather than create your own, this will save you from frustration, waste of money and time, and plenty of trial and error!

Back Garden Chicken Coop Plans

If you're keen on raising one or two chickens while living in the city, these are some basic requirements you need to keep in mind:

- Build your chicken coop on a perfect spot that faces the sun and is well lit.

- Keep 4 square feet of space for each bird inside the coop. The chicken run or outside area of the coop should be at least 10 square feet per bird.

- A triangular shaped chicken coop is a popular design option, plus the tilted roof allows rainwater to drip off without wetting the walls.

- Ensure adequate ventilation and sunlight by installing a window along the south side of the chicken coop so your birds get fresh air, light and keep healthy.

- Build roosts or perches for them to sleep on that are no more than 3-4 feet off the ground, with 9 feet of horizontal space.

- Place a tray below the perches for chicken droppings to maintain cleanliness.

- Install nesting boxes to encourage them to lay eggs, in one place.

- Make sure that you can enter the coop easily for cleaning and collecting eggs.

- Get materials lying around your home – tarpaulin, old wooden logs, PVC pipes, shingles, nails, 50 gallon barrels, wire, but make sure they're in good shape.

- Check out second hand stores for bargains on poles, hinges, roofing material, handles, plywood and lots of other things.

- Build a coop with solid walls so your chickens feel safe and snug.

- Use chicken wire outside the coop without any gaps to keep predators away.

- It's a good idea to construct the coop with an elevation to take care of torrential rains and provide shade during summer months.

- Keep doors and windows south facing to get maximum warmth from the sun.

- Install doors that are secure, open inwards and have a screening system.

- Place feeders 10-15cm above the ground so they can access food and water.

 The Easy Way To Build A Coop
Building a chicken coop is a lot easier if you follow a guide book rather than using guesswork.

A Peek Inside The Coop

Now it's time to think about what you need to put in the coop –

- Nest boxes
- Roosts or perches
- Feeders and waterers

Nest Boxes

Nest boxes are basically boxes where your chicken can make a nest and feel secure, thereby encouraging them to lay eggs. A good size is 15" wide and 15" high, though it can vary slightly.

- Put the boxes a few inches above the ground in a more private place so they can lay their eggs peacefully.

- Fill them with straw or some soft padding at the bottom so the eggs don't crack.

- You can even use wooden crates or old drawers to make nest boxes!

- Chickens enjoy perching in front of their boxes, so build a wooden ledge.

- One nest box is enough for 3-4 chickens.

- While building the boxes, slant the tops since chickens like roosting on the boxes' flat surfaces. You'll need the slanted top or else your chickens might roost on the top while doing their daily job and you'll have lots more to clean up!

- Always build the boxes on a level lower than the perches.

- Try building the boxes side by side or on top of each other to save on space.

Chicken Roosts Or Perches

These are raised platforms for your birds to sleep on. Chickens prefer sleeping in the highest place inside the coop since it makes them feel safe.

- Build the roosts at equal levels using a cross design so they intersect at right angles.

- 2" x 2" battens work well as roosts, though you will need to round off the edges and ensure that the wood is smooth, otherwise the bird may suffer discomfort while perching.

Chicken Feeders And Waterers

These are feeding devices and watering structures placed inside the coop so the hens can feed and drink when they want, saving you time. Make sure there's always fresh water and dry food for the chickens.

Keeping Food And Water Fresh
Ideally, dispensers should be hung at the chicken's height to keep them clean and avoid waste.

Chicken Coop Construction Tips

High Design

Building your chicken coop off the ground is an optional but great idea since it keeps out small, urban predators and stops the floor from getting flooded during rains. You might also like to consider building a ramp leading up to the chicken door for ease of access, plus the elevation will ensure that it stays cool during summer while providing your chickens a shady place during the day. Raising the coop off the ground by 10" using concrete blocks should do the job.

Wired Up!

Never compromise on a strong mesh wire since it is integral to your chicken's protection. Build a high enough fence of chicken wire around the perimeter of the coop and also bury it underground. Place the wire in front of the coop door for extra security and surround the coop with wire netting to prevent predatory birds from snatching away chicks, or prowling dogs and cats from eating the feed!

Making 'Light' Of It!

Light is one of the most important requirements for chickens. While building your coop ensure that it faces the sun so when it gets damp outside it keeps the ground from becoming water logged. A wet and damp environment can be disastrous for chickens causing them to fall ill and leading to bacterial growth inside the coop. You will probably need some type of artificial lighting to keep your chickens warm during winter and there are decent, inexpensive lights available at hardware stores. By providing your hens both artificial and natural light all year round you'll keep them laying eggs regularly.

A Clean Deal

Try the low maintenance, deep litter method. Place 4-8 inches of wood pellets, wood shavings or other bedding on the floor of the coop. Use a rake to stir the chicken droppings every few days so they go into the bedding underneath. As the bedding decomposes it'll shrink, so top it up with more bedding until it reaches 4-8 inches again. This method keeps the odor to a minimum, saves on time and gives you rich fertilizer for the garden and the entire coop needs a thorough cleaning only once or twice a year.

'Tipping' The Scales In Your Favour!

Here are some cost-cutting, time-saving and free-ranging tips for you:

Time

The good news is, chickens need very little time and care but you do need to keep aside some time for critical tasks such as locking them into their coops at night and letting them out in the morning.

You also need to ensure that they get their daily supply of water and feed.

You can clean the coop on a biweekly or monthly basis if you have less flock.

Cost

The initial investment you make might seem on the higher side due to bedding and feed costs, but chickens usually bring in rich dividends and compensate for the cost several times over!

They provide you with their fresh eggs and make great pets.

Free Ranging

Try to give your chickens the pleasure and freedom of free ranging, but always secure the area from predators and neighborhood dogs.

If you don't have enough area where they can free range, build them a secure enclosure for exercising and getting some fresh air. You could block off a section of your backyard so your chickens can roam around freely.

Not only will this keep them healthy, it'll also keep your backyard healthy since chickens eat dead leaves, bugs, weeds, and produce fertilizer.

Add-ons That Make Life Simpler And Save On Time

These are some add-on elements that you might want to consider once you've got the basics sorted out and built your own chicken coop successfully:

Automatic Water

Your chickens need fresh water every single day of the year, so you can place an automatic dispenser inside the coop. or at least make life easier by using larger waterers that hold 5 gallons.

Automatic Food

Install a dispenser that can be hung on the wall of your chicken coop and sends out food every day in specific portions. These hanging feeders reduce food wastage and also keep the mess to a minimum. They are extremely handy if you plan on going out for a weekend, keeping you worry free and your chickens satisfied. If you don't plan on going for automatic food dispensers, another option is to store the chicken feed near the coop for easy access in metal cans with secure lids.

Protection From The Natural Elements

In summer, keep a portion of the coop shaded so your chickens can get away from the sun. Use a windbreak to protect them from strong winds and storms.

Electricity

You can use artificial lights to brood chicks by tricking your hens into believing it's a 28 hour day, instead of a 24 hour one! This'll keep them actively laying eggs all year around.

Tools

Keep a rake or broom close to the coop for gathering up old straw and sweeping it. Also, keep a stock of straw for the nesting boxes ready at hand to make certain that the hens can safely lay their eggs without any risk of cracking.

Nest Boxes

You can also save on space inside the coop by building the nest boxes on the outside instead of inside. This will also save you time and energy since you can feed your chickens from the outside itself! All the best in building a chicken coop with your own hands!

Coop Buying Considerations

If you decide that building your own coop is not for you then you might decide to buy one. If this is your chosen route then many of the points that were discussed in building your own apply here too.

There are many readymade chicken houses available on the market today but care should be taken when choosing the right one for your needs. If price is no object, then you may want to look up one of several manufacturers that advertise in poultry magazines, although this option can be more expensive they will last a very long time and can be made to your own requirements.

The other more common option is to buy one of the many flat packed versions that are available and can be picked up on places like eBay relatively cheaply. In the main they are imported from the Far East, but these days they are very well made and there are lots of styles to choose from. Now you are ready to choose your coop here are a few things to help you make the right choice.

Choosing a coop for your chickens can be a headache. There are so many on the market these days and if you are a novice to the world of chickens it can be so easy to choose the wrong one. This can be an expensive mistake as ready made coops are not cheap.

Chicken Coop Examples

Warning
When choosing a coop it will tell you how many birds it is suitable for. We have found that most of the time they are referring to bantam sized birds and not the normal sized hen, so if it says it's suitable for three to four hens it means it's only suitable for two normal sized hens.

The reasons for having a coop are:

- Chickens need to have a safe and secure place to be locked up overnight away from predators.

- Nest boxes (dark and private to lay their eggs in).

- Somewhere they can shelter during bad weather.

How the coop actually looks is of no concern to the chicken, as long as it covers the main three points above it will be fine.

There are a few other points to take into consideration from a human point of view though, these are:

- How many chickens you have or are intending to have. From experience chicken keeping is addictive and not many of us stop at two or three, so I would always advise to buy the largest you can afford.

- Make sure there is a door at the back of the coop for easier cleaning and general maintenance (the easier you make a job the more likely it is to get done).

- Check how many and the size of the nest boxes inside the coop, and the ease of access for cleaning.

- Roosting perches should never be round poles. These can cause damage to the chicken's feet and a lot of the cheaper coops tends to come with these. Perches can be made from 2"X 1" timber and just chamfer the edges away. The perches should be fully removable as they need cleaning on a regular basis and you will need to place mite and louse powders into the perch holders.

- The Roof. Try to avoid buying a coop with a felt roof. A felt roof is a haven for the dreaded RED MITE; they hide and breed to their hearts content between the felt and timber. The only way to get rid of them once they are up there is to strip the roof off completely. This is time consuming and you will end up putting a new roof on. I always recommend ONDULINE for the roof. It's made from rubber I believe, and is corrugated. It is much easier to spray and keep clean and because it is corrugated it also provides ventilation at the top of the coop where needed.

- The pop hole is the entrance the chicken uses to get in and out of the coop. It should be large enough for the chickens to get in and out with ease and should have a door on it. This door may be one that either drops down (the better one in my opinion), or opens outward. The latter can be a pain as chickens can accidently shut it or the wind catches it and it shut's so when you go to lock your chooks up at night none of them are in the coop. You then have to pick them up and put them in yourself (not nice when it's pitch black, the wind is blowing a gale and the rain is coming down in sheets).

- The Run. You may also want a run to attach to the coop for the chickens to have access to outdoors but still be safe during periods when you are away from home (work, shopping, etc). Most of the ready made runs that you can buy with the coops are never large enough and in my opinion are verging on being cruel to the poor old chooks, so this is something to be aware of when choosing a ready made one. Making your own is the best option.

- Covers. Part of the run needs to be covered so it provides shade for the birds in the summer months and shelter from bad weather in the winter. Also you will need somewhere to protect the feeder from the rain. If the feed gets damp it sours very quickly and can make the birds ill. You will also need space for the drinker as chickens need quite a large supply of clean, fresh drinking water. If you make the run it is best to use a close mesh on the sides and top as it will deter the wild birds from eating the chicken feed and spreading diseases to your flock.

I am not a huge fan of plastic coops, they are never large enough and you can get a condensation build up inside while the birds are roosting at night which is not healthy for the chickens.

They do have ventilation holes but in my own opinion they are not adequate. A lot of companies are selling them as " mite free housing" but no coop is mite free, you will still get red mite but being plastic you can wash and hose them out.

This is the only benefit I can see with plastic coops.

Chookie Checkpoint

Buying a cheap chicken coop can sometimes be false economy, buy the best one you can afford and make sure it is big enough if you plan to get more chickens.

Summary

Well, you should now be in a position to make your mind up about which option is best for you. By using the information provided you can now go and order the right chicken coop to suit your requirements.

With the excitement now building and your coop requirements sorted, in the next chapter we will discuss everything you need to know to feed your hens properly.

Feeding Your Chickens

To ensure that your hens stay healthy and give them a long, healthy and productive life it is essential to give them the correct healthy diet.

I have heard of all kinds of weird and wonderful things that some owners feed to their hens, but in the rest of this chapter I am going to cover exactly what you should, and shouldn't, feed your hens to keep them fit and healthy.

Warning
It is now illegal here in the UK to feed any kind of kitchen scraps, meat, eggs, animal bi-products or any food that has come via your kitchen to chickens or allow access to any of the above.

This is because of the potential for contamination, leading to disease transference and disease risk.

This applies to the domestic keeper as well as the commercial industry and regardless of if the eggs are sold or not.

You can of course feed them left over greens from your vegetable patch as long as it hasn't come via your kitchen.

It is very important to feed your new chickens the correct diet from day one. Their main diet should be layers pellets or layers mash.

Layers Pellets And Layers Mash

Your hens should always be fed on a good proprietary laying mix which can be layers mash or pellets, they are basically both the same just in a different form.

Mash or meal as it is also called, is in a powder form and is fed dry to the hens.

Layers pellets, as the name suggests, are in pellet form and this is my preferred option as I find them more convenient and less messy than mash.

Mash, however, can be more useful if your hens are confined to a run as they take longer to eat the required amount and by staying longer at the feeder this can reduce boredom.

Mash or Pellets
Generally there is no difference in the makeup of mash and pellets and they both contain all the essential nutrients, vitamins and minerals that are vital to your hens' health and to enable her to keep producing lovely eggs.

Which one you use is entirely down to personal choice, but it is a very good idea to ask the person you are buying your hens from what sort of food they are currently being fed and to keep them on the same one.

Feeders

It is important that you use a proper hopper feeder to put your mash or pellets in and these can usually be bought from the place where you get your feed.

Most pet shops now sell feed and feeders as do agricultural merchants and you can sometimes get them from the place you buy your hens from, and of course there are many places online.

A Selection Of Drinkers And Feeders

The feeder should be hung at head height if possible, this enables the hen to still be able to eat comfortably but stops the risk of the hen getting its feet in the feeder and scratching it all over the place.

If you can hang the feeder inside or in the run under a cover, this will stop the feed from getting wet and the possibility of it going mouldy.

You should let the feeder go empty now and again as this will stop the risk of any stale food building up.

Another important reason for using a proper feeder is to give the hens access to the food at all times, they will not get fat on a layers ration and will only take what they need.

When considering which brand of feed to buy, try to choose the best one you can afford that has no artificial growth promoters, yolk colorant, or antibiotics.

If in any doubt ask your stockist for advice.

You should on no account feed your hens solely on corn.

Chickens that are allowed to free range round the garden will supplement their diet by eating an array of bugs, grubs, insects, worms and other such things.

Warning
Before letting your darling little chooks free-range round your garden you may want to consider fencing off your favorite plants and veg patch as there is nothing they like better than to have a good old scratch around your plants looking for bugs.

Or turning your best bit of soil into a nice dust bath. I think that by taking a few precautions you and your hens can live quite happily together in your garden.

Treats

Once you have your chickens you will very quickly fall in love with them and want to give them lots of treats to make them happy, but a word of caution, by giving your hens too many treats and the wrong sort, you could actually be doing them more harm than good.

With that in mind I shall now cover what sort of treats you should be giving to your hens.

Corn

Mixed corn is a great scratch feed to give to your hens when the weather turns cold. Corn should be fed late in the afternoon only; it will help to keep them warm as they roost at night while it is slowly digested.

Chickens will gorge themselves on this type of food in preference to any feed. The mixed corn is not really healthy for them and should only be fed in small amounts.

As they prefer the corn, if too much is fed they will be missing out on essential nutrition and put on extra weight. A fat hen will lay fewer eggs and it will shorten its lifespan. I would suggest only a small handful per hen when the weather is cold.

Just because poultry outlets sell this type of feed it does not mean it's good for chickens!

Do not give corn to young hens under the age of 24 weeks, young hens have an immature digestive system and can have difficulty digesting it.

This can lead to an impacted crop and could be fatal. Long grass and straw can also cause this condition, so keep the grass short on areas where your chickens roam.

Other Treats

Some other treats can include fresh fruit and veg. They particularly like cabbage and other members of the brassica family, greens are very good for them and help to deepen the colour of the yolk.

People who buy eggs from us always remark on how lovely and yellow the yolks are in our eggs. We do not use feed with any artificial additives and the colour of the yolks is down to a good balanced diet.

If you don't grow any vegetables of your own you could always ask your local greengrocer if he has any cabbage trimmings that you could have.

Our local greengrocer saves us a box every week full of trimmings and other fruit and veg that is no longer saleable but perfectly okay for our chickens, it also saves him having to dispose of them.

If your hens are confined to a run, try hanging a bunch of greens up in the run, this will keep the hens occupied and help relieve boredom as they have to work hard for their treat.

They also like chopped carrots, onions, turnip and swede tops. They also like lettuce, but this holds very little nutritional value for them and in large amounts can upset the nutritional balance of the hens' diet.

Pumpkins and other members of the squash family are a great treat for the hens and one cut in half will keep them occupied for some time while they peck at it, eating the seeds and the flesh.

Never feed them bread, pasta, cakes, biscuits or crisps as once again these are no good for them and could cause them to be ill.

Feeders should be cleaned out once a week.

Always feed treats as late in the afternoon as possible. This way they will eat their required amount of layers pellets during the day and it will not upset their nutritional balance.

Grit

You will need to provide your hens with mixed poultry grit as it helps the hens to digest their food, and also for the calcium to help make good strong egg shells.

The grit will consist of a mix of ground oyster shells and small pieces of stone.

It is the small pieces of stone that help the hen grind up and digest their food, as the hen has no teeth it swallows the food where it is stored in the crop, this is located on the chest area and can be seen as a soft lump after the hen has been eating.

The food then passes from the crop to the gizzard where it is ground up and digested.

The oyster shell provides calcium and helps create strong egg shells.

If your hens are free-ranging they may well get enough grit from the soil as they forage, but it is best to offer it to them in a small dish that they can't get their feet in or knock over. If they take it, keep the dish topped up, but if they don't take any off it the chances are they are getting enough from the garden.

Winter Feeding

Hens will eat more during the winter months as they use more energy to keep warm, and as I have already said this is the time of year when mixed poultry corn should be given. It should only ever be used as a winter scratch feed. A small handful per hen is sufficient, and it can be thrown on the ground for the hens to scratch around for it

Do this late in the afternoon and it will help keep them warm overnight.

Water

Chickens can drink up to 500ml of water a day and sometimes more when the weather is warm. Fresh water is very important as the hens also need a certain amount of it for egg production.

Water should be provided in a proper chicken drinker which come either in plastic form or better still, a galvanised metal one. The latter is usually easier to refill and will last a lifetime if looked after properly, they are more expensive though.

The hens like to drink little and often and as they drink the water is topped up by gravity to the drinking bowl.

Drinkers should be cleaned regularly and the water replaced with fresh, daily.

Chookie Checkpoint

A small treat now and again will do your chickens no harm but be careful, sometimes you can spoil them to much and make them ill

Summary

I hope you now understand how important it is to make sure your new hens are fed a good and proper diet to maintain good health and good egg production, and that fresh, clean water should be available at all times.

In the next chapter you are going to start getting really excited as I am going to cover getting your first hens and how to choose the right ones for you, so join me on the next page and we'll get started.

Choosing And Getting Your First Chickens

In this chapter I am going to provide all the information you need to help you choose the right chickens to suit your needs and circumstances.

I am going to cover:

- Hybrids
- Pure breeds
- Bantams
- Ex-battery hens

I suggest that as a beginner you should consider buying your chickens at *point of lay* (POL), this means that they will be around 16-20 weeks old and just about to start laying, although generally hybrids will actually lay their first egg around 22-24 weeks and pure/rare breeds a little longer.

When you buy your birds at point of lay all the hard work has been done for you by the breeder.

When purchasing your chickens you would be well advised to steer clear of places like markets and bird sales as you could end up with poor stock.

The best advice I can give you is to buy from somewhere that has been recommended by a friend, or if buying hybrids, seek out a local agent from one of the breeding companies which can be found in one of the poultry magazines, or of course on the internet.

It is advisable, if circumstances permit, to buy at least 3 hens rather than just 2 because if anything happens to one of them a hen is then not left on her own. They do like the company of other hens and if left on their own they can become very depressed and even lose the will to live.

If buying pure or rare breeds then get in touch with the secretary of the breed society who will put you in contact with the nearest reputable supplier.

A good supplier will also have a good knowledge of chickens and should be happy to answer all your questions.

Always go and check out the place you choose to buy your chickens from and make sure that the conditions they are kept in are clean and the birds themselves look healthy.

They should be bright and alert and moving well, they should have an upright posture and clean fluffy bums. Steer well clear of any that look hunched up or have runny beaks or coughing or sneezing.

After your selected bird has been caught, make sure you have a good look at it before it gets put in the box.

When we sell a chicken here I always take her out and show the customer the bird and check her over and make sure the customer is happy, I also show them how to hold and handle the bird.

Common sense is the key here I think, if you have any doubts at all about a particular bird then choose a different one.

Before I get onto the specific types you need to establish in your own mind the main reason why you want to keep chickens, it sounds obvious but people keep them for many different reasons.

Some reasons could include:

- Pets for the children
- Maybe pets for yourself
- A few hens to provide eggs for the table.
- To provide some colour and decoration for the garden
- To give ex-battery hens a new life

Whatever the reason the following information should help you make the right choice.

Pullets

The term "pullet" is given to a young hen that has not yet laid an egg. *Point of lay* is considered to be from the age of 16 weeks; this means the pullet is coming up to the age of laying for the first time.

It is better to buy your hens at "Point Of Lay" as it gives them time to adjust to their new surroundings, get to know you and settle in before they start to lay. It also means you do not miss out on their maximum laying period in the first year.

All hens will lay throughout their first winter as they very rarely moult in their first year; if they do it will only be a few feathers and may not even be noticeable. This will not be severe enough to stop egg laying.

Hybrids are usually earlier in going into lay at around 20 to 24 weeks of age; this can be earlier or later depending on the time of year. Pure breeds can be a lot older than this before you see your first egg.

Hybrids

Modern hybrids are a far cry from those developed for battery conditions. In the main they have been bred for free range conditions and tend to be a bit heavier in build.

Over many years of selective breeding, hybrids (cross breeds) have been produced that will lay a lot of eggs, typically 280-300 a year, and are now available in many different colours and types.

They are generally very docile and friendly in nature, so are particularly suitable for children as they are easy to handle.

With the different types available it is possible to get brown, dark brown, white and now blue eggs.

If you purchase your hens from a reputable supplier (which you should), they will be vaccinated against most of the common poultry diseases, this is usually administered by drinking water.

The vaccinations will include salmonella, which is a great peace of mind as this could be passed down through the eggs to the consumer.

You will also be happy to know that hybrids are usually cheaper than pure/rare breeds

Hybrids are not so prone to going broody (see frequently asked questions).

On the downside, hybrids will not usually live as long as rare/pure breeds and will not lay for as long as a result.

On the following pages are some examples of the more common hybrids available today.

Rhode Rock

- Bred for over 40 years

- Capable of laying 280-300 high quality eggs a year

- Robust yet docile brown egg layer is highly productive in any management system

Columbian Blacktail

- Rhode Island Red based breed

- Combines all the production and economic benefits associated with a modern hybrid with the traditional good looks of the chestnut plumage

- Hardy and docile it suits any system

Pied Suffolk

- A striking black and white feathered, brown egg layer.

- Large farmyard type fowl with very thick plumage and good body weight.

- Prolific egg production

- Excellent shell quality

- Hardy bird and well suited to our climate

Copper Black

- Copper Black Maran base hybrid
- Produces very high quality eggs
- Large percentage of eggs have very dark brown shells
- An excellent choice for varied colour egg production

Columbine

- Most have crest on top of their head

- Light framed bird

- Great little characters

- Bred from the cream crested legbar

- 80% lay blue/green coloured eggs with the rest pastel coloured

Sussex

- An excellent sex linked utility strain of the very popular and attractive Light Sussex.

- Very good domestic bird

- An eye catching addition to any flock

- Hardy

- Good for beginners

- Fast maturing

As you can see from these examples there should be something to suit everybody's taste.

If you are just purchasing 3 or 4 then you could get different types so they are easy to tell apart.

Now that we have covered hybrids another option for you to consider is pure breeds.

Pure Breeds

There are many different types of pure breed chickens available and the choice is huge as they come in many different shapes and sizes, colours and all kinds of markings and plumage. There really is something to suit every taste.

But a word of caution, some of the more strange breeds may not be suitable for the beginner so I will concentrate on some of the more popular breeds. You may wish to do your own research and take advice from the breeder before going ahead with your purchase.

Pure breeds have a bit of a royal connection as back in the 1800's Queen Victoria started keeping some Cochins, a big fluffy breed that had been sent over as a gift from China.

It then triggered off what was probably the first chicken keeping craze and more and more people started keeping chickens, which led to some of the first poultry shows.

Many of the pure breeds have their own club or society so if you want to get good, healthy examples of your chosen breed you should contact the secretary of the relevant breed club who can put you in touch with a local reputable breeder.

There are also some rare breeds that are on the register of the Rare Breeds Survival Trust, so if you want to help preserve some of the old and rarer breeds, this option might be worth considering.

Here are a few points to consider when thinking about purchasing pure breeds.

Pros:

- There is a much larger variety to choose from than hybrids.
- In general they are more colourful.
- Longer lifespan
- You can get support and advice from the relevant breed club.
- Many different characteristics and personalities.
- Good examples can be exhibited at shows where you can have a great time meeting like minded people.
- You would be doing your bit for conservation of the breed.
- Good for your ego to show off to your friends.
- Although they generally lay fewer eggs than hybrids, they will carry on laying over a much longer period, but at a reduced rate. (A pro and a con).

Cons:

- They are much more likely to go broody
- Making the right choice of breed is essential as some are not suitable for beginners.
- They are usually more expensive than hybrids.
- Not always fully vaccinated.
- Can be more difficult to find the sort you are looking for.

- Some do not lay very many eggs at all.

I shall now list some of the more popular pure breeds available that I have kept myself. As I have said there are many more to choose from, but please do your research properly before making your mind up.

You could of course go for a mixture of hybrids and pure breeds and have the best of both worlds.

Rhode Island Red

- One of the more popular pure breeds that originated from Rhode Island, New York, USA and is the state bird

- A good choice for back garden flocks due to its egg laying capabilities up to 260 eggs a year.

- Very hardy bird ideal for free ranging.

- Good utility bird for meat and eggs.

- Friendly chickens with a good nature, ideal pets for children.

- Lays a light brown egg.

Light Sussex

- A dual purpose bird that originated in England around the time of the Roman conquest of Britain.

- Very popular, docile backyard garden chicken.

- Comes in 8 different colours although the white on is the most common and readily available.

- Another very good layer matching the Rhode Island Red at 260 eggs a year.

- Striking white bird with lovely black lacing around its neck with black tail feathers.

- Lays light brown eggs.

White Leghorn

- A pure white bird that originated in Tuscany, Italy and was introduced to the United States in 1828, from the US they came to Britain in around 1870.

- Very prolific layer of white eggs.

- Very common in many countries of the world.

- Can be very flighty, but are great little characters.

- Lays around 280 eggs a year but can be as many as 300-320.

- Not prone to going broody.

Silver Grey Dorking

- There are other types of Dorking but the Silver Grey is the most common.

- Currently on the rare breeds register.

- Believed to be the oldest breed in Britain and came over with the Romans.

- Takes its name from Dorking, Surrey, UK.

- It has 5 toes, which makes it easy to identify.

- Very friendly, docile and make excellent pets for children.

- Not such a prolific layer as those mentioned previously, but does lay a nice large white egg.

Welsummer

- Originally from the village of Welsum in the Netherlands.

- Friendly and docile.

- Sought after by many for their dark brown eggs.

- Striking rustic red and orange colour.

- Will lay around 200 eggs per year.

As I have said previously there is a huge selection of pure breeds to choose from but the ones listed above are some of the more common breeds and ones which I have kept myself at one time or another.

Bantams

In very simple terms Bantams are a smaller (miniature) version of some of the pure breeds. They share most of the same characteristics but are smaller, typically one third to one quarter of the size of a full grown hen.

Most of the large chicken breeds have a Bantam counterpart and are becoming very popular for the back garden hobby keeper as well as for showing.

Bantams are a very good choice for those that have limited space in their garden as they are a lot smaller compared to a standard hen, they take up less room.

They come in a whole range of colours, shapes and sizes which is another reason for their appeal.

Nearly all bantams are very docile and friendly in nature which makes them ideal for children as pets.

Most are prone to going broody which can be a real pain sometimes as they sit in the nest box all the time, but this can be a plus point if you have some fertile eggs that you want to hatch as they will quite happily sit on the eggs and after they hatch they make great mothers.

In general they lay fewer eggs than their bigger counterpart, and of course their eggs are a lot smaller.

Below are some photos of some bantams that have kindly been supplied by my good friends Cindy and Alan Thompson.

Modern Game

- Originating in England in the late 1800s.

- Mainly an exhibition bird but can become very tame.

- Not good egg layers.

- Comes in about a dozen different colour variations.

Golden Pekin

- Very docile, gentle, decorative and fun loving.

- Good layer for a bantam.

- Make excellent pets.

- Can be very tame and enjoy human company.

Orpington

"Charlie" Our Chocolate Orpington Cockerel

- Fluffy and cuddly and easy to handle.
- Make great pets for children.
- Good layer.
- Different colours available.

Bantams make a good choice if you are after something smaller with lots of colour and are good with children

They lay smaller eggs and go broody very easily.

Ex-Battery Hens

Starting with ex-battery hens is a good and very rewarding way to start keeping hens.

I thought if I spent a little time providing you with some good information on the subject and you choose to go down this route, then at least you will be well prepared.

If after reading my information and you decide to go ahead then I suggest you talk to "The British Hen Welfare Trust" (details in the resource section) who can give you more advice and put you in touch with your nearest coordinator.

First of all let me say, re-homing, looking after and getting your new hens back to full fitness can be a very rewarding experience indeed, when you see your hens pecking at grass for the first time, when their natural instincts kick in, it can almost bring tears to your eyes.

Getting the rewards, however, is going to take a little work on your part and a bit of patience, remember these poor birds have been confined to a very small cage all their lives almost unable to move and with up to 18 hours artificial light to ensure they keep laying well.

When you first get your hens they will not actually be unhealthy but quite a few (not all) will be in poor condition, unfit have lots of feathers missing and generally look worse for wear.

However, the feathers will start to grow back within a few weeks and after only a few months most will be fully feathered again and looking rather splendid.

You should prepare yourself for some heartbreak that occasionally one might die suddenly after initially doing well. Some just can't take the stress unfortunately.

But don't get too hung up on this as the majority will live between one and three years with many living to a ripe old age.

I don't want to get too over dramatic here but these poor creatures have had such an awful life if you can offer them a home you will be rewarded in a way you never imagined.

You will find they are very gentle, endearing, inquisitive and very, very friendly. They will eat out of your hand and follow you around the garden, pecking around your shoe laces, it's as if they know you have given them a new life and all they want to do is repay your kindness.

Housing

Their housing needs are pretty much the same as I have already covered earlier.

Initially you will probably have to coax your hens out of their house as they will not realize they can go outside. You may also have to put them back in at night to start with.

They will probably roost on the floor initially, and don't be tempted to put them on the perches as their legs will be very weak and you may damage them. Patience is the key.

Feeding

Your new hens will have been fed on a powdered mash for their short lives so far so to suddenly put them on layers pellets will be a severe shock to the system as they simply won't know what they are.

It is advisable to keep them on layers mash/meal for a few weeks, and then you can slowly introduce a few layers pellets over a period of time.

However, if you want to provide the best possible nutrition for your hens then there is now a range of Ex Bat Crumbs by Smallholder.

You could then start introducing Ex Bat Pellets as above. This feed has been specially designed for hens from a commercial laying unit.

Introducing To Other Hens

It is very important that when you get your hens home they are kept separate from any existing hens you might have.

It is a good idea if they could be put in a secure run so they can see the other hens, but not have contact with them. This will make the final integration somewhat easier.

Hens have a strict pecking order so prepare yourself for a few squabbles but normally it settles down fairly quickly and everybody knows their place.

Even in the secure run your new hens will establish a pecking order, but don't get too alarmed as it will settle down.

I think I have outlined the main points to be considered before getting ex-battery hens but expert help is on hand at the British Hen Welfare Trust.

Finally, I would like to conclude by saying once you have got your hens settled in, fully feathered and back to full fitness there is absolutely no greater feeling of joy knowing that you have done it and given her a new life, truly wonderful.

Chookie Checkpoint

The British Hen Welfare Trust has a very dedicated team please contact them for more detailed advice.

And Finally

As you can see there is a lot to be considered when getting your first hens, so just to recap:

Hybrids are easy to source, lay lots of eggs and friendly but do not live as long as pure breeds and not so many types to choose from.

Pure breeds are in the main very colourful, lots of different types to choose from but good ones can be difficult to find. Lay fewer eggs than a hybrid but lay over a longer period.

Ex-battery hens are wonderful, friendly birds that can be very rewarding to keep but do require a bit more effort on the part of the keeper, especially initially till they are fully feathered.

Bantams are smaller friendly birds, great for small gardens, good with children but can go broody.

Now you have all the information you need to be able to make the correct choice according to your own circumstances, so good luck and happy hen hunting.

Looking After Your Chickens

Getting Them Home

Before you go to collect your new chickens, it's worth checking with the supplier or breeder to see if they supply a box for you to bring your new birds home in.

Some places will provide a proper cardboard pet carrier for a small extra charge; this is good news as it will be handy to keep should you purchase any more hens in the future, or if you need to take one to the vet. You should expect to pay around £3.00 for such a carrier.

If the supplier does not supply a box you will have to take one of your own. You should be able to pick up an empty cardboard box from your local store or supermarket.

To give you an idea of the size you will need, a crisp box will be big enough for 2 hens. Please make sure you put some air holes in the box so the hens can breathe.

The box should be put on the back seat of your car if possible and not in the boot or they may suffocate, especially if the weather is warm.

If possible, the best time to collect your chickens is late in the afternoon.

Getting Them Settled In

Your new chickens may be a little stressed when you get them home, so they will need to be handled gently and carefully.

Your coop should have already been prepared as previously mentioned, but please make sure that food and fresh, clean water are available.

Gentle remove the chickens one at a time and place them carefully in their new house. Leave them in the house overnight with the pop hole shut, the next morning you can open it and let them out into the run.

Don't be tempted to try and force them out of the house, patience is the key here and you should give them the time to come out by themselves. By doing this it helps the bird to know where it has got to go back to in the evening to roost.

Sometimes they will not realise straight away where they have to go to roost so you may have to put them in yourselves at night to begin with, but they will quickly learn.

It is advisable to keep your new hens safe in an enclosed run for a week or so to get accustomed to their new surroundings.

After this settling in period they can then be let out to free range, by this time they will know where to go back to for food, water and to sleep.

Please always remember to lock your hens up after they have gone to roost as they will rely on you to keep them safe. It is a good bet that the one night you forget will be the night the dreaded Mr Fox will pay you a visit, the aftermath is not a pretty site I can assure you.

Introducing New Chickens To An Existing Flock

At some point you may want to get some more hens, so I thought I would explain that chickens have a strict pecking order within any group and there is usually one "boss" chicken, then everyone else all knows their place from the top to the bottom.

When you introduce new birds to an existing flock there will be some inevitable squabbles as a new pecking order is established and everyone gets to know their place once more.

The best time, if possible, to introduce your new chickens is at night after your existing birds have gone to roost, this helps reduce any bullying, although it may not stop it altogether.

All the birds can then be let out together in the morning. You will need to keep an eye on them for a few days to ensure the bullying does not get out of hand.

It is always handy to have a spare pen or somewhere else to separate the main offender, usually the one at the top of the pecking order.

I recommend that you introduce at least two hen's at a time as this effectively divide's the bullying in half. Also ensure that your coop and run are large enough for your new birds to escape from the worst of the bullying.

Alternatively, and probably the best solution, is to have a separate run alongside your other hens so they can see each other but not come to any harm. They will then gradually become accustomed to each other and you can let them all run together.

Protecting Chickens From Predators

Chickens have a lot of attributes but unlike most animals in the food chain, except for their typical if not initial distrust, they have none for defence. Aside from that, chickens do not move very fast, are noisy, meaty and tasty and that makes them the ideal bird to prey on.

To protect chickens from predators and other animals, try to observe the following:

Introduce human smell. The scent of humans is very repulsive to animals. It has often been claimed that the reason that man is the least to be preyed upon is due to human smell. There is not much study to support this but the fact is man will only be preyed upon when a predator is starving and there is nothing else available.

To do this, hang bags of hair and used clothing inside the chicken coop and around the perimeter of the fence and also near the entrance. Another way is to save your pee in a bottle and spray it around the perimeter fence.

How you will discourage predators from your premises will depend much on the predators that are in your area. Different predators use different methods. Consult with the animal control or the local authorities in your area.

Here in the UK we have foxes, mink, weasels, stoats and badgers amongst others, but in different parts of the world you could have wild dogs, coyotes, wolves, raccoons, snakes, but it shouldn't be too hard to find out the predators that are likely to be around where you live.

An electric chicken fence may also be ideal. Outside of these, remove places and clear spaces where predators could hide. Having dogs around will discourage most predators from getting near the place, every night when I lock my girls up I take my 3 dogs down with me and they have a good run round the field, spreading their scent as they go.

Build sturdy chicken coops. Build the chickens living spaces free from gaps and holes. If the flooring of the chicken house is made from slats, install wires underneath to prevent predators from digging from underneath. Cover weak posts with wires to prevent them from being bitten through and lock up the chicken hutch without fail when the chickens are roosting in their coops.

Prevent access. Predators will dig underneath a fence if they cannot jump over it. When building the fence, ensure that it goes at least 10" or more below the ground to discourage digging. See to it that there are no weak points either in the fence or in the chicken house itself.

Provide barriers. When the fence is made from chicken wire, bury planks that are at least 8" deep into the ground, also put footplates near the fence.

Make the height of the fence at least six feet high to prevent foxes from jumping over. Leave the top of the fence rough for added measure. Generally foxes could jump as high as their length. There are foxes though that could jump more than that so leaving the top of the fence rough could catch if not scrape their underbellies on it.

Daily Routine

After a good night's sleep your chickens will awake at first light and may jump down from the perches in readiness to be let out.

It is your first job of the day to let your chickens out for their daily forage, you do this by simply opening the "pop hole" this is the small door by which your chickens go in and out of the coop.

If you have removed the drinker overnight this can be emptied cleaned and refilled with fresh, clean water and put back in so the chickens have access to it. Also check the feeder and refill as required with pellets or mash.

It should be your aim to keep your chickens in as clean and healthy environment as possible, so after attending to the feeder and drinker you should inspect the inside of the coop and remove any chicken droppings from the previous night.

By doing this daily you avoid a build up of poo which is not healthy for your birds and reduces the possibility of any smells, so your birds and neighbours will be happy. The droppings can easily be removed with a small hand-held shovel or a garden trowel. The droppings can then be put on your compost heap where they will do a world of good.

Once your birds are out and about it is a good time to stand and observe your hens, by watching them you will get to know them and be able to spot any problems they might have or if one of them is ill.

Try talking to your birds as this will help form a bond with them and help them to become tamer.

Chickens tend to eat the majority of their daily food intake during the morning, so hold off on any treats you might want to give them until the afternoon; otherwise they will fill up on the treats and will not get the required amount of their proper layers ration which they need to keep them in prime condition.

Now for the best bit, if your chicken coop has a nest box attached to it (which it should have), sometime during the morning they will go to the nest box to lay an egg. This can take about 20 minutes or sometimes longer and can be accompanied by some gentle clucking and some more when she has finished.

Over a period of time you will get to know the usual time your chickens tend to lay their eggs and they should be collected as soon afterwards as you can. Children really love collecting the eggs and when my grandchildren come to stay it is the first thing they want to do.

After a while your chickens will become quite tame and soon start to follow you round the garden. They are very inquisitive and if you are working outside they will come to see what you are up to. If you are having a meal outside in the warmer weather, take care as some of the chickens may well jump onto the table to see if you have a treat for them.

Sometimes if your chickens are free ranging they might lay their eggs outside of the nest box, so if you notice that some of your birds don't appear to be laying its worth checking around the garden and under bushes to see if they are laying outside.

At the end of the day your chicken have an inbuilt habit to take themselves off to roost at dusk or as it starts to get dark, so make sure the pop hole is left open otherwise they will roost on top of the coop or the nearest tree or bush, they are then open to attack by predators such as the dreaded fox.

Just as it starts to get dark you need to go down and shut the pop hole and make sure the chickens are secure for the night.

Remove any drinkers from the coop itself as they can cause a damp atmosphere, which is not good for your birds. If you have a feeder outside the coop this also needs to be removed to discourage vermin. They can then be checked and put back the next morning.

Your Beautiful Garden

A word of caution if your chickens are going to free range around the garden:

Chickens love to scratch around to find bugs and insects to eat and they will eat some of the slugs for you as well. The thing is though, the chicken cannot tell which your prized plants are and which are not.

So to avoid having your beautiful garden destroyed by your chickens scratching around and dust bathing in your flower beds or vegetable patch, it is a good idea to give some protection to those areas that you don't want your chickens to go on.

This can be done by simply netting off the plants you don't want damaged or you could place some chicken wire around the base of the plants.

Handling Your Chickens

As your chickens become used to you it should not be too difficult to pick them up. You may want to do this simply to give them a cuddle and a stroke or you may want to pick one up that you suspect might be ill or have some problem.

When catching and picking up a bird you should never grab it by the legs as you could easily damage them or dislocate one of the joints.

You should pick the bird up with both hands, one either side of the body, this way the bird will not come to any harm and by taking a firm but gentle hold you will stop any flapping of the wings.

Once you have hold of the bird, bring it up towards your chest and put its legs through your fingers so you still have hold of her. She should then be sitting in the palm of your hand with the head facing your elbow.

By holding the hen like this she will feel safe and secure and will settle down and be quite happy for you to stroke her, or indeed inspect her if you suspect she has some kind of a problem.

If your chicken is proving difficult to catch you could use a net, we sometimes use my sons fishing net. You could also try crouching down and gain the birds confidence by offering a treat.

How to hold a chicken

Try not to make a desperate grab for them otherwise you may cause some harm or pull some of her feathers out.

Cleaning And Maintenance

I have already said previously that droppings should be collected on a daily basis to provide a healthy environment for your chickens to live in, but once a week the whole coop will need a thorough clean.

Weekly Clean

You should aim to clean out your chicken coop once a week. This needs to be a thorough clean whereby everything should be removed scraped, cleaned and replaced.

If the perches are removable (which they should be), they need to be taken out and inspected, scraped, and cleaned. You should check the ends of the perches and where they are located for any visible signs of red mite (to be covered in the Problems chapter).

If there are any signs of red mite it should be treated as specified in the Problem chapter.

All the soiled shavings from the floor or droppings board need to be removed, the floor can then be sprayed with a suitable disinfectant such as Smite and then when dry the new shavings can be put in.

The same procedure should be followed when cleaning out the nest box.

We always add a sprinkling of Diatomaceous Earth (Diatom Powder) to the shavings and also sprinkle some around the perch ends and any cracks in the timber. Add a sprinkling to the nest box as well.

The reason we do this is to act as a deterrent to a red mite invasion as they do not like the Diatom powder so this will significantly reduce the risk of your cop being invaded by these pests.

You may also add Diatom powder to the area where your birds dust bathe. Chickens love to dust bathe and will carve out big holes as they scratch about and get all the dust through their feathers. The Diatom acts as a deterrent to mites and lice as once again they do not like it.

If you do not have any Diatom then louse powder will do the same job but is more expensive.

Drinkers And Feeders

Whilst carrying out your weekly clean you should give your drinkers and feeders a good scrub out to get rid of any germs or bacteria. These can then be refilled with fresh water and food.

Maintenance

The extent of the maintenance you will need to carry out will to some degree depend on the setup you have.

The following should really be checked daily, but if not at least weekly.

If you have a run attached to the house you should check to make sure all the mesh is secure and not coming away from the frame.

You should check around the base of the run to see if there are any signs of digging, if there are it might mean a fox has been trying to dig his way in.

If you find evidence of digging it might be a good idea to put paving slabs around the base of the run to deter foxes and the like.

If your birds are free ranging you should do the same checks on the perimeter fence of your garden.

If using electric fencing to contain your hens it needs to be checked regularly to ensure it still works.

Apart from the fencing the chicken coop itself needs to be checked. First of all ensure all locking bolts hinges and fittings are secure and ensure the coop is sound and secure, no holes in the roof or any boards coming loose.

Lastly, check around the outside to make sure there are no signs of vermin trying to chew their way into the house. Rats in particular are notorious for this.

One way of helping to prevent this is to have the house off the ground. If the house is on the ground and there are any rats about then there is nothing a rat likes better than to tunnel underneath the coop.

By raising it off the ground it doesn't give the rats a place to hide.

Seasonal Considerations

Spring And Summer

As spring comes around it brings the start of longer days which means it will get light earlier in the morning and it will get dark later in the evening, so this is something to bear in mind with regards to letting your hens out and also locking them up at night.

Quite often on a warm summers evening I have gone down to lock up the chickens around 10pm only to find they were all still out and about scratching away without a care in the world.

Just keep returning till they are all safely in bed and make sure you don't ever forget to lock them up.

With the extra daylight your hens will begin to start laying more eggs, this is great news and can herald the arrival of the cake making season.

Unfortunately, the warmer weather can also herald the arrival of some mites and lice which live on the hen or the dreaded red mite which live in the coop. If using Diatom powder as mentioned previously then you may be lucky to keep them at bay but in any case you need to inspect the house and birds regularly and treat as per the instructions given in the Problems chapter.

You will need to keep an eye on the chickens water drinkers as during warm weather they will tend to drink a lot more, you should refill as required during the warm weather.

You should ensure the chickens are provided with some shade, they might find this under a bush or tree but if not you should provide some for them. Even a patio umbrella would do.

Below is a photo of a natural living willow sculpture I made which will root and grow and in turn provide shade for the summer and also a dust bath.

My Living Willow Sun Shade And Dust Bath

They love to dust bathe and will create their own in a bit of soil. You could of course make them one by making up a timber frame and filling it with sand and earth and some louse powder or Diatom. It is a good idea to cover the dust bath to stop any rain turning it into a mud pie.

During periods of very warm weather you should ensure there is sufficient ventilation in the chicken coop, this can be done in most cases by simply opening the sliding vents.

If your coop does not have any sliding vents you could cut a hole towards the top of the coop and staple some fine mesh over the hole.

Summer is a great time to be with your chickens and I have a table and bench down in the chicken field, it's great fun to sit there with a cup of tea and while away a few hours watching the chickens and their antics.

Autumn And Winter

With the arrival of autumn and the shorter days, and as a result less daylight hours, this will mean a drop in egg production by your hens. In the autumn and winter your hens will lay fewer eggs.

Some pure breeds may well stop laying altogether during this time while hybrid hens should continue to lay, but at a reduced rate.

Your hens are less likely to be bothered with lice and mites at this time of year as they do not care for the cold, so this is a small bonus.

During wet weather you should keep an eye on your bird's feet as they may start to get a build up of mud on their feet and in particular you may spot balls of mud on their toes.

This should be removed straight away and can be easily done by bathing the foot in warm soapy water and gently working the mud free from the toes. Do not try to prise it off while dry as you may damage the toe itself, patience is key here.

If you have chosen to keep some of the hens that have feathered feet then once again you need to keep an eye on them and treat as before with warm soapy water.

If you are worried about your chickens freezing during the winter, keep in mind that you only have to take minor precautions to keep them warm.

Remember, chickens normally acclimatize themselves to cold weather. In fact, their physical constitution is more tolerant to cold than to heat. The body warmth they get from simply huddling together during cold weather can go a long way towards keeping them warm for most of the winter.

However, it doesn't mean that it's safe to neglect the environmental conditions that determine the well-being of your chickens during the cold months.

Heat conduction plays a critical role in the wintering of your chickens. Placing a bed of sawdust or bundles of straw in the coop (assuming the coop is big enough) helps in keeping them warm just in case huddling together is not good enough to handle the cool temperature.

A coop that is dry and free of draft (but still ventilated) is very essential to maintaining reasonable heat within the shelter. One thing to avoid is keeping the pop hole shut since chickens love to go outside and exercise every once in a while, even during winter.

Make it a point to clear the coop's surroundings of snow in order for your chickens to have the luxury to venture outside whenever they feel the urge to do so, they do not like the snow and unless you clear an area for them they are likely to stay inside.

Proper feeding is very important during a chicken's winter days. Corn is a good supplementary diet since it provides internal warmth, corn should be given as a winter scratch feed late in the afternoon so it sits in their crops and generates some extra heat as they slowly digest it overnight.

Of course water needs to be provided daily just like in summer days. I highly recommend using a hard rubber dish or washing up bowl for the fact that it's relatively easy to remove the ice without breaking the dish.

Providing roosts is also vital in avoiding your chicken's toes from freezing. A roost made out of wood is always better than metal or plastic because wood doesn't conduct cold, but in fact you should never use plastic or metal poles as roosts anyway.

The roost should also be wide enough so that the chicken's feathers can cover the toes and be able to provide warmth into them.   Combs and wattles on chickens can be a big problem since extreme coldness can cause frostbite.

Gently rubbing Vaseline onto the combs and wattles can be a big help to alleviate this particular problem.

You will also need to keep an extra eye on your hens for signs of any coughs, colds or general symptoms of being unwell.

Chickens do not like wind so you should provide shelter from it as cold winds can get under the feathers and chill the hen's body. Most chickens do not like the rain much either but each time it rains here, there always seem to be a few of my hens who want to tough it out in the rain for some reason, while the sensible ones are all safely huddled up in the warm and dry.

Coping With Severe Heat And Cold Conditions

Severe Heat

In warmer climates, like some parts of North America such as Arizona, California, Florida and the Deep South, the temperatures can get up to 40 degrees Celsius and higher.

Also in Australia many regions experience very high temperatures.

When the weather is extremely hot, as well as following the advice already given I have a few extra tips for you.

1. Try installing a 12 volt fan in the coop or run. The good thing about using a 12 volt fan is that it can be run off a car battery. The cooling breeze will be of great benefit to your chickens.

2. You can give them some ice cold watermelon as a treat.

3. Put a shallow dish of cold water in the run, a plastic flowerpot saucer is ideal. I know some people who put ice in the water as well. You will need to change the water at frequent intervals if possible.

4. You could (if finances allow) install a cold water misting system, this can be put up in the run.

As chickens were originally jungle fowl you will be surprised how tolerant of heat they actually are.

Warning
Always ensure there is some sort of shade available where your chickens can shelter from the direct heat of the sun.

Severe Cold

Here in the UK we usually get at least one very cold period during the winter when snow and ice and freezing conditions make life a bit miserable for our beloved chickens.

Helpful Tip
Always think and plan ahead don't wait for problems to arise.

In other parts of the world such as Canada winters can be very severe indeed, so here are a few extra tips to make life a little easier for your hens.

1. Heated mats are now generally available to place your drinker on and help prevent it from freezing; you can also buy special watering stations that are designed not to freeze. Remember chickens can go longer without food than they can without water.

2. You could place straw bales around the coop to help provide insulation, just ensure the bales are not touching the coop but are placed a few inches away all round.

3. In extremely cold conditions you might consider putting a heat lamp in the coop. A word of caution though, make sure you use one that has a protective mesh screen and it is securely fixed out of reach from the hens.

Instead of an infrared bulb you could try using a dull emitter bulb as this will provide heat without light. This type of lamp is designed to provide heat without getting too hot.

A timer switch could also be fitted to make life easier.

4. Frostbite can be a problem if there is lots of snow about and a howling wind, so if possible try and make a covered area for your hens which should have a good thick layer of straw on to provide some insulation for them to walk on.

Summary

We have now covered everything you need to know to be able to get started and keep your chickens nice and healthy and for you to really enjoy having your hens roaming around the garden. I have tried not to make it too complicated as this may put some people off, really there is not much to it and you will learn as you go along.

Remember you can always ask us a question on our Facebook page if you have a problem or are stuck on something. This can be found at http://www.facebook.com/ilovekeepingchickens

In the next chapter I am going to cover some of the poultry problems that you may encounter, so turn the page and I'll begin.

Poultry Problems And Diseases

I would just like to say before we get into the nitty gritty of this chapter, that many of the problems and diseases I am going to talk about can usually be prevented simply by good husbandry.

What do I mean by this? I simply mean that if you look after your hens well, make sure they are cleaned out regularly and fresh food and water are available at all times and then you will be repaid by having good clean, healthy stock.

All you need to do is follow the advice already given in previous chapters and you will greatly reduce the risk of getting any problems.

I should of course point out that buying healthy, fully vaccinated hens in the first place will also help. If you buy cheap hens that are not of good health then you are asking for problems further down the line.

I think I can sum it up by saying that diseases and problems are not natural to well kept chickens.

As this is a book with the beginner in mind I am not going to list every problem and disease that chickens can succumb to as in all probability you will never encounter most of them anyway. I am only going to cover the most common problems and diseases.

Recognising A Sick Hen

Just before I start I thought it would be a good idea to outline what to look out for in a healthy and sick hen.

Healthy birds are bright-eyed, alert and interested. Signs of poor health include:

- Hunched posture.
- Head tucked under the wing.
- Reluctance to move.
- Hiding in corners.

Please consult your vet if you are concerned about your hen's health.

It is also advisable to have somewhere safe to isolate a hen when you need to as at some point you will have a need to do this.

So let's begin now by starting with some of the more common ailments and problems.

Warning
As soon as you spot a sick hen you will need to treat it straight away or seek help from your vet. Don't think the hen will recover by itself, its your job to look after them. This chapter will help you

Chicken Parasites Causes And Treatments

Chickens in general are a hardy lot, but they are also very susceptible to various chicken parasites, infestations, and diseases. All of this could be avoided very easily provided the symptoms are recognized early and treatments are done swiftly. Not acting on it soon enough could cause infestation that could contaminate the entire flock.

Causes Of Infestation In Chickens

- Overcrowding chickens produces stress that results in lowered resistance against diseases, it also makes the chicken prone to parasitic diseases and infections.

- Introduction of new birds into the flock without first quarantining the new birds is one of the most common sources of infestation. When additional chickens are needed the best way is to quarantine the new flock first in a separate cage for two weeks and examining and treating them for possible infections before being introduced to the main chicken house.

- Poor sanitation breeds different kinds of bacteria that the chicken is susceptible to. The chicken house must be cleaned regularly from manure, dirt, dampness and waste food to insure that the chicken house is sanitary.

Common Chicken Parasites And Their Treatments

Lice

While lice do not actually bite the chicken but instead eat dead skin, chicken are very uncomfortable with it that results in the chicken pecking at themselves which causes irritation and wounds. When other chickens see the blood it attracts their interest so they would peck on the chicken also resulting in depression and death. Lice are usually transmitted by introducing other birds that are infected to the chicken house. To treat lice, spray the infected chicken with sulphur based dust sprays. Malathion solution baths are also effective.

Red Mites

Red mite are the scourge of chicken keepers so I am going to cover this in some detail as especially in the summer months nearly all us chicken keepers will get an attack at sometime and we get more questions about this subject than anything else.

Red mite are the vampires of the chicken world.

This tiny parasite hides in the daytime in every nook, cranny and crevice inside the chicken house.

It will come out of hiding at night just after the chickens go to roost. They crawl along the perches and then onto the chickens to have a blood feed. When they have fed they crawl back to their hiding places and repeat this process every night until they are spotted by the chicken keeper and duly dispatched. They breed and reproduce at an alarming rate and the numbers run into millions in a very short space of time.

It does not take long for the birds to become anaemic with more and more mites feeding off them each and every night. Once the birds are anaemic it lowers their immune system and leaves them open to infections and diseases. The birds will die if the problem is not solved or kept under control very quickly.

Preventative Things You Can Do

A number of preventative measures can be taken in the form of powder treatments, e.g. Red Mite Powders and Diatomaceous Earth. These can be put into nest boxes, on the perches, the perch holders and under the bedding on the floor of the coop, basically everywhere you can manage to get it. Make sure the mite powder you buy to dust the birds themselves in is suitable for this purpose as some are just for the coops.

Warning
Do not become complacent and think because you are using powders you will not get red mite. You will! They will just hide and breed in the places where you cannot get to with the powder!

Just one of these places is between the felt and timbers on the roof of the more traditional type of coop.

Don't be fooled with claims from makers of plastic coops that they remain mite free. The mites don't care if it's made from wood or plastic! The only advantage of plastic coops is there are fewer places for them to hide and they can be washed with detergent and hosed out. Therefore the mites are washed out every time you clean the coop and the numbers are not going to build.

Try not to use straw in the coop; it's a haven for red mite. Wood shavings (dust free, animal grade) are a better option.

Spraying

There are numerous sprays on the market and the one's we use here are Total Mite Kill and Poultry Shield. We swop the use of these every week to help prevent the mites building up a resistance to one particular spray. This is done every week in the warmer months after cleaning and in conjunction with the powders mentioned above.

The best you can ever hope to achieve is to keep the numbers of mites under control as you could rid the coop of them one week and the following week a new infestation will make themselves at home.

They are not fussy about who they feed from either, they will bite and feed from us as well given the chance! They can also travel into your home on your clothing and on the eggs.

Red Mite can live for at least 8 months without feeding, so do not put infected bedding on the compost heap. Burn it if possible. If you cannot do this, double bag it and sprinkle some Diatom or mite powder inside the bag, tie securely and put into the dustbin.

A customer of mine last year had been disposing of the chicken bedding into the garden waste recycling bin and did not realise he had red mite. His wife opened the lid a couple of days later to put some rubbish in and screamed for him to come and see the bin. It was teeming with red mite and they were all over the lid and crawling down the outside of the bin as well!

So please check your coops every week for this horrible parasite and as soon as you see it, act quickly to stop the problem escalating.

Scaly-Leg Mites

You will find scaly-leg mites in between the scales of the leg of the hen, with the toes and legs covered in white flaky matter. Once they have penetrated the scales, the scales would lift and will cause great irritation in the chicken and even lameness.

The mites are spread from bird to bird so it is very important to treat immediately you spot it to stop it spreading from bird to bird.

Unlike the red mites, scaly-leg mites come from infested ground.

To treat the problem you can use one of the sprays available these days, especially for scaly leg mite, they are widely available from most pet stores and the larger chicken supply stores.

I have found the best treatment is Surgical Spirit.

First of all wash the birds legs with warm soapy water then take a small jar and fill with surgical sprit, then holding the hen firmly dunk the leg into the jar right up to the hock joint.

Keep the leg immersed in the jar for 20-30 seconds then repeat the procedure with the other leg.

As the scales lift, do not be tempted to try and pick them off as they will then bleed rather heavily. The leg may take up to 12 months to get back to looking normal.

Chicken Sour Crop

A chicken's crop is just below its neck and at the centre of its chest. This is the chicken's food storage and also where the first stage of digestion takes place. Sour crop is mainly seen in hens and is caused by a fungus called Candida albicans.

This fungus develops inside the crop and in turn will cause the crop to get bigger and fill up with some rather evil smelling liquid.

Detection and Symptoms

You would know if the chicken has sour crop if there is a bulge at the centre of the chest of the chicken (often bigger than a golf ball) making the chicken very uncomfortable and moving the head in a funny sort of way. When you open the beak, there is often a sour, foul smell. When you touch the chickens crop and there is that soft and squishy feeling, sour crop is setting in if it is not yet impacted.

What complicates this is that even when the chicken appears to be lethargic; it will still try to eat even when the crop is full, then the chicken suffers more.

This should not be confused with an Impacted Crop, where the lump is hard. Impacted crop is caused by the bird eating too much hay, straw or long grass, this causes a blockage, hence the build up of food causing the lump, this means little or no food can pass.

Prevention of Sour Crop

Unfortunately, not much is really known why hens pick up the fungus so not much can be done to prevent it.

A healthy chicken with a crop that is working well will have emptied the crop overnight. If the crop has not, there is something wrong with digestion. To aid digestion, the chicken feeds on grits. Grits are bought in any farm and poultry supply store, the grit is then mixed with the chicken feed that aids digestion.

Normally, healthy foraging chickens will swallow small pebbles. They know what to select and what is good for them. However, if the chicken is not let out of the coop for long periods, they miss this digestion aid. Another thing that is common to most animals is to eat a particular grass for a particular illness. When the chicken has sour crop, the chicken feels the illness and will forage for grass. This often complicates the sour crop as long strands of grass are harder to digest.

To prevent the onset of sour crop, check the chickens once in a while as the crops are likely to be empty every morning before they feed. Once a month, mix one teaspoon of apple cider vinegar to every litre of water in the chicken's water supply. When you do, make sure you buy the apple cider vinegar from a poultry shop or your local chicken accessory supplier and not those sold in the supermarkets.

Apple cider vinegar is cold compressed and retains all the beneficial vitamins and minerals that are good for your chickens. Apple cider vinegar bought from the supermarket is distilled, so many of the vitamins and minerals are removed during the process.

Treatment

The treatment of sour crop is a bit of a messy job.

Holding the hen upside down you should try to make it vomit as much as you can by rubbing the lump with your hand until it is as empty as you can get it. It is not a pleasant job but needs to be done for the good and benefit of your hen.

After nearly all the crop is empty you should administer some "live yogurt" this can easily be done with the aid of a plastic syringe.

Try doing this a couple of times a day for 2-3 days and you will find that the yogurt will clear up the fungus.

Egg Bound

A hen that is egg bound is not able to pass an egg properly and it is either just stuck inside or may be just visible.

This is caused by simple cramp whereby the muscles just seize up which in turn stops the egg from passing. This needs to be treated quickly.

Treatment

You could apply some olive oil around the vent in the hope this will ease the situation or more experienced keepers will try enemas with olive oil or liquid paraffin, but I would not advise trying this as a beginner.

In my experience I have found that by bringing the hen indoors in the warm for a day will normally suffice.

Simply place the hen in a cardboard box or pet carrier with some straw in so the hen feels secure and relaxed, make sure the box has enough ventilation holes.

Bring the box indoors and place by a warm radiator or heater. The egg will then normally pass after a few hours.

Worms

Nearly all hens will pick up worms, some more than others. The amount of worms they pick up will to some degree depend on the environment that they are kept in. Chickens shouldn't be kept on the same piece of ground for too long and should be moved frequently if you only have a small garden.

It is not always obvious if a hen has worms, although picking a hen up that is very light could be an indication that worms are present and sometimes you may see them in the birds poo.

In any event I would recommend that you worm your hens twice a year as a matter of course.

Treatment

There are some natural wormers on the market, although I cannot comment on these as I have never used them.

The only wormer licensed for poultry is called Flubenvet. It is very safe and will kill off ALL worms found in poultry including lung worm and gape worm.

I have always used Flubenvet and it has been very effective over the years and I have never really had a problem with worms.

Flubenvet is available to the public from your vet or from many online retailers; it is a white powder and comes in a 60 gram tub. This tub is enough to treat a 20 kg sack of feed. Clear instructions are on the back of the tub.

How To Treat

The hens need to be wormed for a period of seven days.

1. Calculate how much feed your hens will eat for seven days, generally a hen will eat approximately 1kg a week, it is much easier if they are on layers pellets (which they should be).

2. Put this feed in a bucket and add a SMALL amount of oil, such as cooking oil or olive oil. For large amounts you may need to split and then repeat the process.

3. Mix the pellets with your fingers so that they all get a coating of the oil.

4. Read the instructions and sprinkle the appropriate amount of the worming powder over the pellets, then mix up once more.

5. The powder will then stick to the coated pellets and not end up at the bottom of the feeder where it will not be eaten.

6. Top up your feeder with the coated pellets and ensure the hens stay on the mixture for seven days.

I think this is all I need to cover in this book. There are of course other ailments and diseases that chickens can succumb to but I think I have covered the more common ones.

What I would like to say is that if at any time you think you have a sick hen then you should seek help from your vet if you are in any doubt.

You could always post a question on our Facebook page (details in the keep in touch and resource section) to see if we can help with your problem, if we can't we would advise you to take the hen to your vet.

And Finally

So now you know about the more common ailments that can affect chickens you may be thinking oh my god what am I letting myself in for.

In answer to this all I would say is, I have a duty to let you know about these things and you should not let it deter you from getting started in this truly fantastic hobby.

At the risk of repeating myself, I would emphasise that if you look after your chickens properly and carry out good husbandry, then the risks of them getting any parasites or any ailments will be greatly reduced.

Chookie Checkpoint

Contrary to general opinion chickens do not look after themselves....*you* need to look after them!

Frequently Asked Questions From Our Facebook Page

Following on from our previous chapter I thought it would be a great idea to list some of the questions that have been posted on our very popular Facebook page "I Really Love Keeping Chickens", and obviously the answers as well.

In the main the questions have come from newcomers to the hobby just like yourself. I thought this would be of great benefit to you as you will be able to see what problems other keepers have had and how to overcome them.

So without further ado, let's get started with our first question which comes from Edith Miles from the UK.

Question 1

One of my hens has gone broody and sits in the hen house all day being anti-social. Is it best to just leave her to get on with it? She comes out when we go into their enclosure and rattle the box of corn! This allows us enough time to clean out the house and remove the solitary egg. We're only getting ONE egg at the moment as apart from the broody girl, one of the others has simply stopped laying and we have only three little hens in total :-(Any suggestions, comments or advice?

Great question from Edith, here's the answer.

Answer

You really need to break her of this broodiness as they can lose a lot of condition during this period. Deny her access to the nest box at all times or use a "naughty cage" as we call it. This is a dog cage under which is four bricks one placed at each corner.

No tray on the bottom just the bare wire with no bedding but you need to put in food and water. She needs to be kept in the cage for about 5 days, maybe longer if she returns to the nest box after you let her out.

This is not cruel but very necessary as the hen could otherwise loose an awful lot of condition by sitting in the nest box for a long time, as she will not eat or drink properly or go to the toilet often enough. It can take hens months to recover from this and some even die.

Broodiness is caused by a hormone change within the bird and all hens do it, although hybrid hens are less likely to do it after the first year. Your other hens should be in full lay at this time of year (June).

Question 2

Our next question comes from Lee Haunch from the UK who recently (June 2012) bought some 17 week old hens from us. His hens were using the nest boxes instead of using the perches. This is actually a very common question.

I was wondering if you might be able to help me. The hens I bought from you recently are doing really well but at night they keep sleeping in the nest boxes instead of using the perches, what can I do to make them roost on the perches? Thanks.

Answer

Young hens sometimes need teaching to use the perches. You need to do this once it is dark by placing them on the perch one by one. Once it is dark they will not move. If you do this for a few nights they will eventually do it themselves.

It is never a good idea to let hens sleep in the nest box as they still poo while they are asleep.

When they then start laying (especially if it's early in the morning) they will lay the eggs into the poo which is not good as the egg shell is porous and can absorb the bacteria.

Question 3

The next question comes from Advark Ptang Ptang concerning poisonous plants.

POISON... Hi, can anyone inform me if Laburnum pods and seeds are harmful to chickens? A friend is thinking of making a run and this tree is in the area.

Answer

Laburnum is toxic to all animals, especially the pods and seeds. Chickens are usually very sensible when it comes to poisonous plants, trees, bushes, etc. but I personally would not take any risks as an accident may happen. I would advise your friend to sits the chickens as far away as possible and probably cut the tree down.

Question 4

This question comes from Dagmara Shannon who says some of her hens are not laying.

My 4 hens are now around 1.5 year old, they have been laying very well over the winter, but in the last few weeks eggs have been scarce, I'd normally get on average 20-25 eggs a week, now struggling to get 10. They don't look like

they are moulting, they are a nice weight, the skin is clean and pale, they are going about their business as usual, they get layers pellets and extra grit, plus treats, and they are free range, so they find other things as well.

They have always laid in the nest boxes. How long will it last? Are they having a break? Is it possible they are laying outside somewhere? There has been one or no egg even when I let them out late (they have a big indoor pen. Is there anything else I should look out for? Thank you.

Answer

My money is on parasites causing this. Check for red mite in the coop, lice and mites on the birds themselves and worm them with Flubenvet. Clean out the coop and drench it with red mite killer and get Diatom all over the inside of the coop, do this every week during the warmer months.

Also dust the birds with Diatom and repeat every 4 days. Cut out the treats and just leave them with their layers pellets for a week or two, so they are replenishing the nutrients they have lost.

It will take a few weeks to right itself but when done they will start to lay eggs again.

Question 5

Eva-Marie Tordoff from California asks the next question about a wild bird eating her hen's eggs.

A bluejay is eating my hen's eggs :-(Any suggestions??

Answer

You could try putting a lot of pot eggs or ping pong balls in the nest boxes. This may confuse the bluejay and it will get fed up of pecking away and not getting anywhere. You will also need to collect your hen's eggs as soon as they are laid. You could also try shredding a black bin liner and pin this over the pop hole it will not deter the hens from going in but it may deter the bluejay. Good luck.

And Finally

This is just a selection of some of the common questions that we get asked, I hope you now know that you will not be alone during your chicken adventure and we are always here to help. Do pop along to our Facebook page and post up a question if you're stuck.

I always say there's no such thing as a silly question – the only silly thing is not asking it when you need help!

Closing Thoughts

Well I hope you have found this book useful and I would like to think it will be a good reference for you in your future journey into the wonderful world of keeping chickens.

I take a great interest in hearing from all our readers and I would be delighted to hear how you get on, so please send me your success stories. You can do this by email via the contact form on our website or via our Facebook page.

Many people have been asking me to write this book for some time and now it is done I hope it is all they wished for, and if it enables you to now go out and join the merry band of chicken keepers then I think I have accomplished my mission.

If you have any suggestions on how I could make future editions better then please let me know.

Good Luck

Mark ☺

http://www.chickens-for-sale.com

http://www.facebook.com/ilovekeepingchickens

Keep In Touch

The great thing about modern technology and in particular the growing use of social media means that it is very easy to stay in touch.

I would encourage you to stay in touch to let us know how you and your chickens are getting on from time to time. By staying in touch you can also feel free to ask us any questions you have or maybe post a few photos of your new chooks, we would love to hear from you.

Our Facebook page has over 6000 followers and growing so come and join the chicken gang.

Twitter for us is relatively new but I have an ever increasing following.

Here are the links

http://www.facebook.com/ilovekeepingchickens

http://www.twitter.com/meetmarkburrows

Need More Help?

I would like to assure you that as you have invested your hard earned money in this book you will be looked after. We have built our business on the good old fashioned ethics of "nothing is too much trouble for our customers".

I really want to help you, so if you have a problem or need some help then please contact us via any of the links I've shared with you.

Resource Section

I thought it would be a good idea to give you some useful resources that will help you with your purchase of chickens and equipment, and also a list of informative websites.

I have only been able to provide resources for the UK, USA, New Zealand and Australia, but some are applicable worldwide.

Resources UK

Suppliers Of Chickens And Equipment

Chicken House Poultry
Point of lay chickens and one stop poultry shop for all your poultry needs under one roof

Redlynch Farm
Main Road
Stickney
Lincolnshire PE22 8EQ

Tel: 07834 618242
Email: enquiries@chickens-for-sale.com
Website: http://www.chickens-for-sale.com

Glencroft Poultry
Suppliers of point of lay pullets, ducks and housing.

Hipswell Road
Catterick Garrison
North Yorkshire
DL9 4AY

Tel: 01748 832786
Email: glencroftpoultry@btinternet.com
Website: http://www.glencroftpoultry.com

Newland Poultry
Hens, ducks poultry supplies and equipment

Newland Grange
Stocks Lane
Newland
Malvern.
Worcestershire
WR13 5AZ

Tel: 01684 216257
Email mail@newlandgrange.com
Website: http://www.newlandpoultry.com

Flyte So Fancy
Huge range of poultry equipment and supplies. Superb range of chicken coops and houses

The Cottage,
Pulham
Dorchester
Dorset
DT2 7DX

Tel: 01300 345229
Email: info@flytesofancy.co.uk
Website: http://www.flytesofancy.co.uk

Martins Wood Chickens
Point of lay hens poultry supplies and equipment.

Martins Wood Farm
Deanland Road
Ripe
East Sussex
BN86AR

Tel: 01323 811877
Email: info@martins-wood-chickens.co.uk
Website: http://www.martinswoodchickens.co.uk

Omlet
Famous Omlet plastic Eglu housing large range of poultry equipment and supplies

Omlet Ltd
Tuthill Park
Wardington
Oxfordshire
OX17 1RR

Tel: 0845 4502056
Email: info@omlet.co.uk
Website: http://www.omlet.co.uk

Regency Poultry
Huge range of poultry supplies and equipment

Merrydale Farm
Enderby Road
Whetstone
Leicester
LE8 6JL

Tel: 0116 2866160
Email: info@regencypoultry.com
Website: http://www.regencypoultry.com

The Domestic Fowl Trust
Point of lay hens poultry equipment and supplies.

Station Road
Honeybourne
Evesham
WR11 7QZ

Tel: 01386 833083
Email: clive@domesticfowltrust.co.uk
Website: http://www.domesticfowltrust.co.uk

Useful Poultry Magazines

Practical Poultry
Includes very useful breeder directory for the UK

Website: http://www.practicalpoultry.co.uk

Your Chickens
Fantastic magazine for all chicken keepers

Website: http://www.yourchickens.co.uk

Poultry Organisations

Poultry Club Of Great Britain
Fantastic site with up to date information.

Website: http://www.poultryclub.org

Rare Breeds Survival Trust
Up to date information about rare breed poultry

Website: http://www.rare-breeds.co.uk

British Hen Welfare Trust
Friendly expert advice on rehoming ex-battery hens

Website: http://www.bhwt.org.uk

Resources USA and Canada

Readers from the US and Canada should find the following resources useful.

Poultry Supplies And Equipment

USA

Bowles Poultry Supplies
Hatchery and poultry supplies

312 O'Connor Rd.,
Lucasville, OH 45648

Tel: 740-372-3973
Website: http://www.feathersite.com/Poultry/BRKHatcheries.html

Smiths Poultry Supplies
Everything you need to keep poultry

14000 West 215th St.
Bucyrus, KS 66013

Tel: 913-879-2587
Email: smith@poultrysupplies.com
Website: http://www.poultrysupplies.com

My Amish Goods Truly
Superb chicken coops and poultry supplies

Tel 1-800-365-4619
Website http://www.myamishgoods.com
Email amishgoods@gmail.com

Premier 1 Supplies

Suppliers of everything for the poultry keeper and homesteader

2031 300th Street
Washington IA

Tel: 1-800-282-6631
Website: http://www.premier1supplies.com

Kemps Koops Online Poultry Supplies

Poultry supplies and chicken coops

3560 West 18th Ave.
Eugene, OR 97402

Tel: (888) 901-BIRD (2473) [Toll-free]
Website: http://www.poultrysupply.com
Email: info@poultrysupply.com

Poultry Man Supply Company

General poultry supplies and equipment

520 Agawam Rd.
Winchester, KY 40391

Tel: 859-737-2636
Email: info@poultrymansupply.com
Website: http://www.poultrymansupply.com

My Pet Chicken poultry supplies
Poultry, poultry supplies and equipment

1253 Springfield Ave. #163
New Providence, NJ 07974

Tel: 908-464-3239
Email: info@mypetchicken.com
Website: http://www.mypetchicken.com

Poultry Suppliers

The following link is a superb resource page that will give you details of poultry suppliers from all over America. You should of course check out the supplier before purchasing your hens.

Website http://www.feathersite.com/Poultry/BRKHatcheries.html

Canada

Fanciers Speciality Canada
Poultry supplies

143 Snyders Rd. W.
Baden, Ontario
Canada N0B 1G0

Tel: 519-634-5607
Email: fanciers_specialty@hotmail.com
Website http://www.goldbook.ca/baden-on/birds-equipment-supplies/fanciers-specialties-co-100303/

Berry Hill Limited
Poultry equipment and supplies, also farm equipment.

75 Burwell Road
St.Thomas, Ontario
Canada N5P 3R5

Tel: 800-668-3072
Email: info@BerryHillLimited.com
Websitehttp://www.berryhill.ca

Seven Oaks Manufacturing and Sales
Large and small scale poultry equipment.

Seven Oaks Manufacturing and Sales Alberta
12245 Fort Road
Edmonton, Alberta
Canada T5B 4H2

Tel 780-471-1657

Organisations

American Bantam Association
Great information for anyone interested in keeping bantams.

http://www.bantamclub.com

American Poultry Association
Dedicated to promoting and protecting standard bred poultry.

http://amerpoultryassn.com

Useful Poultry Magazines

Backyard Poultry
Great magazine for poultry keepers with US breeders directory.

http://www.backyardpoultrymag.com

The Poultry Magazine
Another good source of information about poultry.

http://www.thepoultrymagazine.com

Home Grown Poultry
Great website and magazine all about keeping poultry.

http://www.homegrownpoultry.com

Resources Australia And New Zealand

Poultry Supplies And Equipment

Readers from Australia and New Zealand should find the following resources of use to you to help you purchase your poultry supplies and equipment. There are more listed in your local poultry magazines

Brookfield Poultry Equipment pty Ltd
Queensland mail order Australia wide, everything you need for keeping poultry

Brookfield
QLD 4069

Tel: 07-3374-3031   Mobile: 80458 775313
Email: info@brookfieldpoultryequipment.com
Website: http://brookfieldpoultryequipment.com

Blue Hills Poultry Stud
Specialists in rare breed poultry

Blue Hills Rare Breeds Stud
c/o Helidon Post Office 4344
Grantham and Helidon
South East Queensland
Australia

Tel: 0433 179 844

Email info@rarechooks.com.au
Website http://www.rarechooks.com.au

Royal Rooster

Static and mobile chicken coops and poultry supplies delivery throughout Australia.

PO Box 242
Cockatoo Valley
SA 5351

Tel: (08) 8524 6625
Website: http://www.royalrooster.com.au
Email: info@royalrooster.com.au

Australian Poultry Breeders Directory
A searchable index of breeders by region.

Website: http://australianpoultry.net/breeders/index.php

Rent A Chook
Unique site where you can rent the equipment and chooks before you buy, also great information and very helpful.

Kennards Self Storage
497 Victoria Road
Gladesville

Tel: 0409 246 651
Email: chooks@rentachook.com.au
Website: http://www.rentachook.com

Blue Mountain Coops
New Zealand specialist in providing top quality coops and tractors.

57 Bushyhill Street
Tapanui
West Otago
9522
New Zealand

Tel: 03 204 8828
Website: http://www.bluemountaincoops.com

Poultry Valley And Lifestyle
New Zealand chickens poultry equipment and supplies.

337 Mangawhara Road
Hoe-O-Tainui
Tahuna
Morrinsville

Tel Mobile: (021) 114 8050
Email: service@poultryvalleylifestyle.co.nz
Website: http://www.poultryvalleylifestyle.co.nz/

Useful Websites

Backyard Poultry
Full of great information on all aspects of keeping chooks including breeders list.

Website: http://backyardpoultry.com

Poultry Central
Similar site to the above but for New Zealand

Website: http://poultrycentral.co.nz

Living Greener
Solid advice and information for those wishing to keep chooks in Australia.

Website: http://www.livinggreener.gov.au/waste/kitchen-food-waste/keeping-backyard-chickens